YOUR KNOWLEDGE HAS VALUE

Bibliographic information published by the German National Library:

The German National Library lists this publication in the National Bibliography; detailed bibliographic data are available on the Internet at http://dnb.dnb.de .

Imprint:

Copyright © 2003 GRIN Verlag, Open Publishing GmbH
Print and binding: Books on Demand GmbH, Norderstedt Germany
ISBN: 9783668344129

This book at GRIN:

http://www.grin.com/en/e-book/343567/the-importance-of-language-and-culture-in-the-l2-classroom

Ian Akbar

The Importance of Language and Culture in the L2 Classroom

GRIN Publishing

GRIN - Your knowledge has value

Since its foundation in 1998, GRIN has specialized in publishing academic texts by students, college teachers and other academics as e-book and printed book. The website www.grin.com is an ideal platform for presenting term papers, final papers, scientific essays, dissertations and specialist books.

Visit us on the internet:

http://www.grin.com/

http://www.facebook.com/grincom

http://www.twitter.com/grin_com

The Importance of Language and Culture in the L2 Classroom

How shall I talk of the sea to the frog,
if it has never left his pond?
How shall I talk of the frost to the bird of the summerland,
if it has never left the land of its birth?
How shall I talk of life with the sage,
if he is prisoner of his doctrine?
Chung Tsu, 4th Century B.C. (Fantini n.d., 26)

Judging from the above quote, it would appear that being able to understand another person's viewpoint is essential for effective communication. As the perceptions of most human beings are shaped by culture, the most important contribution intercultural communication studies have made for second language teaching is to increase instructor's awareness of the intricacies of managing a multicultural or a monolingual classroom in a foreign learning context, improving teaching and classroom quality for second language students. In support of this argument, this paper presents a brief background on the influence of culture on language, the benefits of studying L2 for cultural acquisition, the importance of recognizing different cultural motivations for L2 acquisition, intercultural differences that lead to misunderstandings and poor learning/teaching, the prevalence of ethnocentrism, and lastly, methods and approaches that may be useful in second language teaching.

Kaplan (1966) was the first author to develop a deterministic hypothesis, suggesting that people from different linguistic and cultural backgrounds organize discourse differently, as a reflection of their native language and culture. (Gonzalez, Chen & Sanchez 2001) Culture through language, thus, both reflects and affects one's worldview, serving as a sort of road map to how one perceives, interprets, thinks about, and expresses one's view of the world. (Scheu &, Sanchez 2002; Landis 2003, 283) Therefore, culture, among other things, affects how one speaks, reads and writes.

Through L2 study, it is believed that students gain a knowledge and understanding of the cultures that use that language. However, intercultural communication studies show that in order to achieve higher developmental levels in ESL/EFL learning, students need to understand the socio-cultural and pragmatic norms of a particular cultural way of thinking. (Gonzalez, Chen & Sanchez 2001) Research indicates that explicit instruction in cultural pragmatics (Goddard 2002) helps students make sense of the values, attitudes and communication norms taken for granted in many language textbooks, oral presentations and letter writing. (Lo Bianco, Liddicoat & Crozet 1999, 135) Studies also demonstrate that understanding the reasons for the behaviour of L2 speakers enables learners to accept cultural differences more easily and thus, creates a more positive attitude towards the target language.

Studies also show that the needs of different learners must be considered and must reflect different approaches in the L2 learning environment. For example, in a case study examining the motivations of Japanese college learners, the most significant motivations for ESL/EFL turned out to be; a wish for foreign travel; the desire for greater contacts with foreigners; English media use, personal development; and interest in cultural comparison. Low value was placed on learning English for instrumental reasons. (McClelland 1998, 48) For the teacher, once the exact nature of the learner's orientation toward the goal of learning English has been clarified, they are in a better position to decide about which strategies to utilize for promoting motivated behaviour. Ideally, these findings can then be used to inform the design of the syllabus and classroom procedures, so that the needs and interests of the students are better fulfilled. (McClelland 1998, 7) In this way, intercultural communication studies are significant in identifying the motivations of various types of learners and in assisting the development of appropriate strategies to achieve communicative competence.

In addition, studies have proven to be very useful in illustrating differences that exist in turn taking, degree of directness, attitudes to the acceptability of disagreement and direct criticism, forms of address, verbal and non-verbal feedback, appropriateness of topics and adjacency pairs such as in greetings, apologies, compliments, requests, leave taking, etc. Different conversational styles are generally, culturally determined. Thus, an awareness of different styles and preferences can help prevent negative evaluations of ability and personality for instructors, as well as students. In fact, it is believed that most of the current learning in an intercultural classroom should be built around incidents of cross-cultural misunderstanding. (Scheu & Sanchez 2002) Instructors should make second language students aware that native speakers may not always be prepared to accept the validity of differing styles of communication which may result in communicative attempts being misunderstood or rejected. Students should be prepared for this possibility being careful not to take such behaviour personally or be discouraged by it.

Since it is likely that teachers and students will have different cultures of learning (i.e., behavioural expectations based on previous classroom experience), differences in norms of behaviour may lead to 'systematic and recurrent miscommunication in the classroom', resulting in an environment that is not conducive to learning. This applies not only to students' behaviour (or misbehaviour) but also teachers' performance. (Kato 2001, 54; Scheu & Sanchez 2002) As students' perceptions about teaching and teachers clearly reflect their own culture of learning, it can be said that understanding cultural differences is one way of improving teacher effectiveness. (Kato 2001, 63) With the awareness that students come from very different cultural backgrounds which have an effect on the learner, that is, Chinese and Japanese students often do not speak out as they are from collective societies that value the group over the individual, a teacher can be more sensitive to their needs.

Intercultural communication studies also note that that many of the materials and methodologies used in second language teaching are often highly culture bound and many teachers take it for (Lo Bianco, Liddicoat & Crozet 1999, 127) granted that these are the most advanced and effective materials and methodologies. This approach has been widely criticized as ignoring reality. If teachers do not clarify underlying assumptions, contempt and hostility may result on the part of the learner who applies his own cultural framework as a yardstick. (Lo Bianco, Liddicoat &, Crozet 1999, 128) Teachers should be aware that the inappropriate application of L1 cultural norms in an L2 context can impede learning. However, learners do need to understand the cultural values and communication patterns preferred in the L2 society so that they are aware of societal expectations and reactions. (Lo Bianco, Liddicoat & Crozet 1999, 130) Studies have helped to develop various theoretical approaches as tools which can serve to illuminate cultural differences to both teachers and learners and overcome ethnocentrism.

Broad frameworks, which researchers have identified, can aid in the interpretation of behaviour and communicative intentions in intercultural interactions. These include: collectivism versus individualism, high vs. low power distance (or hierarchical vs. egalitarian), achievement vs. ascription, universalism vs. particularism and high context vs. low context cultures. These frameworks work best when seen as a continuum on which cultures can be placed depending, for example on the extent to which a culture values the group more highly than the individual and vice versa. (Lo Bianco, Liddicoat & Crozet 1999, 133) For example, the widespread use of first name in Australian English can be better understood as an expression of the high value placed on egalitarianism in an individualistic culture. (Lo Bianco, Liddicoat & Crozet 1999, 135) These frameworks can be useful in aiding instructors in cultural comparison through the L2 in the educational setting.

Researchers discussing the need to teach culture in the language classroom suggest that the best method is to compare the socio-cultural and pragmatic norms of the learner's first language with that of the target language and for teachers to act as cultural mediators and to explain the differences explicitly using a meta-cultural language, e.g. differences in thanking behaviour between the Japanese and the English, etc. (Lo Bianco, Liddicoat & Crozet 1999, 131) Natural Semantic Meta-language researchers predict that in all languages it is possible to express meanings equivalent to I, YOU, SOMEONE, SOMETHING,

PEOPLE, DO, HAPPEN, THINK, SAY, KNOW, WANT; GOOD, BAD, BIG, SMALL, THIS, WHEN,

WHERE, BECAUSE, CAN, IF, NOT, and LIKE, in specific syntactic contexts. These meanings,

known as 'semantic primes', are easily recognizable and easy to learn and could and

should, according to Goddard (2002), form part of the early syllabus of L2 learners.

Studies indicate that semantic explications and cultural scripts allow one to draw

connections between broad cultural themes, key lexical items, proverbs and common

sayings, linguistic routines, etc. Essentially, cultural scripts are phrased in simple, non-

ethnocentric terms. Cultural scripts are not intended as descriptions of how people

behave, but rather as claims about what 'people think' about how to behave (how to

speak, how to think, how to feel, etc.) in different cultures. (Goddard 2002) For

teachers, the awareness that many languages are able to express equivalent meanings

indicates that such meanings can be taught and recognized by L2 learners.

Intercultural communication studies indicate that teachers should also stress individual

differences among students and the role of personality, while not dismissing the role of

culture in the classroom. (Landis 2003, 297) In addition, language teachers should

encourage students to always ask questions about who the people interacting (or writing)

in exercises are, for what purpose the language is used and in what context. These

questions ensure that language texts are understood within their cultural, personal and

circumstantial dimensions. (Lo Bianco, Liddicoat & Crozet 1999, 115) Conversation

should be presented in the classroom in a naturalistic fashion (Landis 2003, 296), i.e., by

using unscripted videoed conversations to preserve the natural features of conversation.

In utilizing unscripted or naturally occurring conversations, it is then possible to show

ESL learners how conversationalists interact, maintain face, what social strategies they employ and how spoken English is used. (Lo Bianco, Liddicoat & Crozet 1999, 148) Studies are therefore useful in demonstrating that the introduction of cultural materials in language classes should be limited to those items that are most closely related to the actual speech act.

In addition, studies demonstrate that the amount of cultural materials to be introduced in the L2 classroom is influenced by the level of instruction and the range of uses to which the language is to be put. The Council of Europe's 'threshold method' where the goal of language instruction is to allow the learner to cope with a society as a foreign visitor, is an example of this approach. (Lo Bianco, Liddicoat & Crozet 1999, 67) Differentiation is also considered an effective way for teachers to offer meaningful instruction delivered around challenging content and designed to meet the needs of students at their appropriate levels and to help them achieve maximum growth. (Theisen n.d.) Teachers should also continuously acquiring new knowledge regarding best practices in ESL and share that knowledge with colleagues. (Montecel & Cortez 2002) Professional development is essential if teachers are to improve their effectiveness in L2 classrooms.

Intercultural communication studies most effectively illustrate that language teachers need to go beyond monitoring linguistic production in the classroom and become aware of the complex and numerous processes of intercultural mediation that any second language learner undergoes. The increasing heterogeneity of today's classrooms reflects cultural, linguistic, cross-generational, immigration, and interethnic diversity.

Accommodating this complex diversity demands a fundamental rethinking of the purposes, curriculum, goals, instruction, and intended outcomes of teaching. As demonstrated above, intercultural communication studies serve to prepare instructors for this formidable challenge by identifying how cultural differences influence the teaching and learning in the classroom and by suggesting possible methods and approaches to improve L2 instruction and acquisition. Studies identify the negative prevalence of ethnocentrism in teaching materials and methodologies, how intercultural differences can lead to misunderstandings and poor learning/teaching, and how important different cultural motivations are for L2 acquisition. Since learning about culture requires an intellectual effort, perhaps the L2 teachers' most difficult task is balancing the need to learn about a language with the need to learn the language itself. Teachers require support for these efforts and professional learning to ensure multiculturalism in the classroom becomes a resource and not a limitation.

BIBLIOGRAPHY

Fantini, Alvino E. (online), 'A Central Concern: Developing Intercultural Competence.
pp. 26-42, retrieved 8 to 12 Sept. 2003 from – UNE electronic database.

Goddard, Cliff. (2002), Cultural scripts and Semantic primes: New Tools for Language
teaching and Language Learning, Keynote address for Global Forum on Mind, Culture
and Drama in Language Study at the University of Wisconsin-Madison, Feb., received 26
Sept. 2003 from –Kyung-Joo Yoon, Instructor LING 453, UNE.

González, V., Chen, C. and Sanchez, C. (2001 online), 'Cultural Thinking and Discourse
Organizational Patterns Influencing Writing Skills in a Chinese English-as-a-Foreign-
Language (EFL) Learner' *BRJ Online Bilingual Research Journal,* Fall, Vol. 25, No. 4,
retrieved 11 Sept. 2003 from -- http://brj.asu.edu/

Kato, Kumi. (2001 online), 'Exploring 'Cultures of Learning': a case of Japanese and
Australian classrooms' *Journal of Intercultural Studies,* Vol. 22, No. 1, 2001, retrieved 8
to 12 Sept. 2003 from – UNE electronic database.

Landis, David. (2003 online), 'Reading and Writing as Social, Cultural Practices:
Implications for Literacy Education' *Reading & Writing Quarterly*, Vol. 19: 2817307,
retrieved 8 to 12 Sept. 2003 from – UNE electronic database.

Lo Bianco, J., Liddicoat and Crozet. 1999. *Striving for the Third Place; Intercultural Competence through Language Education.* Language Australia, Melbourne.

McClelland, David. 1998, 'An Investigation into the Socio-psychological Orientations of Japanese College Students Learning EFL' *TESOL*, pp. 1-69, retrieved 8 to 12 Sept. 2003 from – UNE electronic database.

Montecel, M. R. and Cortez, J. D. (2002 online), 'Successful Bilingual Education Programs: Development and the Dissemination of Criteria to Identify Promising and Exemplary Practices in Bilingual Education at the National Level' *BRJ Online Bilingual Research Journal,*

Spring, Vol. 26, No. 1, retrieved 11 Sept. 2003 from -- http://brj.asu.edu/

Scheu, D. and Sanchez, J. S. 2002, 'Asymmetrical cultural assumptions, the public self and the role of the native speaker: insights for the expansion of intercultural education in foreign language teaching' *Studia Anglica Posnaniensi*, pp. 255(24), retrieved 8 to 12 Sept. 2003 from – UNE electronic database.

Theisen, Toni. (1999 online), 'In the Aftermath of Unz' *LOTE CED Communique,* Issue 6, retrieved 8 to 12 Sept. 2003 from – UNE electronic database.

YOUR KNOWLEDGE HAS VALUE

- We will publish your bachelor's and master's thesis, essays and papers

- Your own eBook and book - sold worldwide in all relevant shops

- Earn money with each sale

Upload your text at www.GRIN.com
and publish for free